# AIRCREW
## IN
# WARTIME

### PERSONAL EXPERIENCES
### by
### NORMAN FIDLER

Published by
STRANRAER AND DISTRICT LOCAL HISTORY TRUST

ISBN 0-9542966-4-8

© 2006 Norman Fidler

Published by
Stranraer and District Local History Trust
Tall Trees
London Road
Stranraer DG9 8BZ

# Introduction

After I left the RAF in 1946 I was kept busy in the furniture business in Stranraer and Newton Stewart and my life in the RAF became something in the dim past to be remembered only occasionally.

At about the time that I retired in 1989 I met up with two of my comrades, Robert Proudley and Bill Boddington, with whom I flew in 22 SAAF Squadron during the war, and we discussed old times and all the exciting things that happened to us when we were young fellows aged 20 to 22 all those years ago. Then a few years ago I was invited to join the local branch of the Aircrew Association and met with and exchanged reminiscences with other men who had flown as aircrew during the war.

This made me start to think that I would like to record my experiences during the war in the hope that my recollections would interest my family and, maybe, others. In late 2005 I started, and I asked an Aircrew Association colleague, Dennis Sawden of Newton Stewart, who had written several books, if he would help me get my story into print. I am pleased to say that Dennis kept me to my task and, with his aid, what follows is the result of labours at my PC during the winter of 2005/2006.

March 2006                                                                 Norman Fidler

*Sergeant Norman Fidler*

# Outbreak of War

I remember well sitting in our living room with my parents and brother Stuart and hearing the broadcast by the Prime Minister, Neville Chamberlain, on Sunday, 3rd September, 1939, announcing the outbreak of war against Germany. At that time we did not realise how close to disaster the country had become. In 1941, I joined the Stranraer Squadron of the Air Training Corps where the CO was Mr Macdonald, the Rector of Stranraer High School. Mr Sutherland, a science teacher at school, was one of the officers on the squadron. During my time as a cadet, we visited the nearby airfield at RAF West Freugh, which was a busy flying unit and I had a flight in a Handley Page Hampden over Lochryan.

After the war had been in progress for two years, I decided that I would apply to join the RAF when my turn came to be called up for war service. At that stage I had no particular interest in entering RAF aircrew, because I didn't think I had the right academic abilities or was cut out for such exacting duties. At the age of 18 years, like everyone else I was called to register for military service in early 1942 and attended at Rosefield Mills, Dumfries, travelling there and back easily by train, on the main line that then ran from Stranraer to Carlisle and London. I must have passed the medical examination A1 as I was then interviewed by a Squadron Leader who read out a long list of RAF trades — engine fitter, wireless operator, driver, flying control, etc — and then he asked me what I would like to train to be. I had to select something immediately, so I chose wireless operator. The RAF agreed and this became my fate.

## Called Up

On 12th August, 1942, just a month after my 19th birthday, I received my calling up papers to the RAF together with a travel warrant and the information that I should report to an address in Princes Street, Edinburgh. On the train were other recruits all going to the same address. More joined the train along the way making a total company of about 20 young men, all a little fearful of what lay ahead and thankful to be among others in the same circumstances. The address in Princes Street turned out to be what had been a small shop. Here we sat an intelligence test, had many forms to fill in and questions to answer. We were sent off to the Music Room to be sworn in. We became full members of His Majesty's Royal Air Force with the rank of Aircraftman Second Class (AC2). I paid a shilling for a bed in a serviceman's hostel off Princes Street. I received a travel warrant and the next day travelled to Padgate, an RAF station in Lancashire. At Padgate I was issued with the RAF uniform, I said goodbye to my civilian clothes and bundled them up into a parcel and posted them off home. I also received my first experience of RAF food, RAF bunk beds and being shouted at by RAF corporals.

## Recruit Training

A couple of days later, after a short train journey, I arrived in Blackpool. Together with squads of other recruits, I was marched out of the railway station and with six others was billeted in one of the boarding houses where I lived for a few months. The middle-aged couple who ran the house were very kind indeed, treating us like sons. We had a full breakfast, three course lunch and high tea. My memories of the recruit's course in Blackpool (square bashing) are not bad. Although the corporals and sergeants bellowed at us 'Get your hair cut, are you a poet?' 'You are the worst lot of recruits I have ever seen.' 'You march like a lot of pregnant WAAFs.' 'You may have broken your mother's heart but you won't break mine', etc., we soon realised that these were routine remarks directed to all recruits and were not personal. We had our hair cut like convicts. We learned to march, to stand to attention, to salute, to put our trousers under the mattress to make a crease, to polish our buttons and cap badge and to clean and use a Lee Enfield rifle. One of the sergeants was Sergeant Matthews who turned out to be the famous Stoke City footballer Stanley Matthews. Twice a week we were marched to the Derby Baths for a shower and a swim. There were three NAAFI canteens where one could have a cup of tea for a penny and sometimes get a bar of chocolate for two pence. There were also many canteens run by generous voluntary organisations such as the Salvation Army and the churches

Although the tower of Blackpool Tower was closed, the zoo, aquarium and ballroom below were open. It was wonderful to be in the Tower Ballroom and see the organ rise up from below, with Reginald Dixon playing and then see hordes of servicemen with their partners swarming onto the floor. Although there were many like me who had never learned to dance, one could always pick up a girl and, with an arm round her waist, push her round the floor and try to think of something interesting to say. With all the exercise and physical training and good food I put on half a stone. My pay was 3/- per day. With deductions for Post War Credits etc, I received 2/6 pence a day, 35/- a fortnight (£1.75) — maybe that was all we were worth! Towards the end of the square bashing, we began the wireless operator's course. We had to learn the Morse Code and how to receive and send messages. We spent long miserable hours in periods of forty five minutes until at last we could receive Morse at four words a minute. This part of the course was now completed. I was sorry to leave Blackpool. The Blackpool people were very good to the airmen in their midst. We were given fourteen days leave which I spent at home.

## Ground Wireless Operator's Course

After leave I was posted to RAF station Madley, No 4 Radio School, a few miles north of Hereford. Madley was a wartime camp with the huts and sites dispersed all around the aerodrome. It was quite a long walk from one place to another. Here I had to learn all about wireless transmitters and receivers, batteries, valves and bring my Morse up to 22 words a minute and learn Procedure. The course took a few months. I had known nothing about wireless before the course, so I had to buckle down and study hard to keep up. At the end of quite a long day, I had to spend at least an hour every night going over the notes. I passed the wireless operator's course and was issued with a 'Sparks' badge to wear on my arm and also received a welcome 1/6d a day extra.

At the end of the course, announcements were made of an invitation to wireless operators to volunteer to train to become aircrew as wireless operator/air gunners. At that time during the war, aircrew were looked upon as gods; heroes who were brave and fearless. Never thinking that I could ever be included in such a body, I volunteered. The day came when I had to stand before the Aircrew Selection Board, a body of about eight high ranking officers with lots of medals on their chests and blue rings on their arms. Somehow or other I must have satisfied them, because I found I had passed and was now an aircrew cadet and was entitled to wear a white flash in my forage cap.

## First Posting - RAF Millom

During the fourteen days leave that followed I was able to show off my hard won badge to anyone who was interested. Then I was posted to RAF Station Millom in Cumbria as a ground wireless operator. The station was about a mile from Millom at Haverigg. (A few years ago I returned to see the old camp and found that the aerodrome and huts had disappeared and in its place was H.M. Prison Haverigg, all high wire fences and grey huts.) The station was, in my time, a training school for navigators. The planes used were Ansons — 'Faithful Annies' — which would take off every night if the weather was suitable. The student navigators would have to plot a course round Scotland and, all being well, direct the planes correctly to arrive back to base all in one piece. I was one of the ground wireless operators in the Signals Office. Our job was to keep in WT contact with the Wireless Operators in the planes as they flew round the course, which took about four or five hours.

I quite enjoyed this job and it was good practice for what was to come, as my Morse improved a lot. All the staff in the Signals Office were female except the corporal and me. We had a wretched system of 'watches', the equivalent of four hours on and two hours off for two days then being off for 24 hours on the third day. But it was springtime. I had my bike, and, sometimes, with other chaps took the train to Windermere and cycled round the area. On one occasion I went with the girls on our watch to the nearby shore and swam in the sea. After a happy few weeks at Millom, I was posted back to Madley to commence the next part of the aircrew course.

## Wireless Operator (Air) Course

I arrived at Madley in June 1943. My rank was still AC2. We had to learn the workings of two sets of transmitters and receivers, the T1154/R1155 and another and be able to repair or adjust them on the ground and in the air. We had to learn how to cope with the electrics on the planes, the accumulators, batteries and aerials. What was most essential was knowledge of Procedure: these were strict rules to adhere to for calling up other stations and addressing them. We learned how to tune in to ground stations and back tune on to their frequency and communicate with them. Then we had to use this knowledge in the air. My first flight was on 23rd July 1943 in a de Havilland Dominie; a twin engined biplane crewed with a pilot, a Sgt Jackson, an instructor and three trainees. We had a few flights in Dominies learning the basics then advanced to flying in Percival Proctors, a small single engine monoplane with just room for the pilot and one trainee. Each trainee was on his own with a project to complete each time he flew. The projects became more difficult as time went on. I became proficient at calling up the base, sending and receiving messages, plain language and code, using the fixed and trailing aerials and the direction-finding aerial. There was never any time to waste as there were always a number of small planes buzzing about with each one containing a WOP trying to get his message across in the short time available. I had 27 short flights at Madley between 12th July and 10th October 1943, passing out as a Wireless Operator/Air. I was posted to RAF Mona in the Isle of Anglesey to start my next course.

# Gunnery Training

At Mona the instructors were not ready for us for three or four weeks, so we were 'volunteered' to do odd jobs on the station. With four others I had to help the gardener, an RAF corporal. He was in charge of a field where he grew produce for the camp. There were endless rows of vegetables to hoe to keep free of weeds, but we looked forward to digging up potatoes, cabbages, etc. and taking them in the wheelbarrow to the WAAFs in the cookhouse and getting a cup of tea and cake as a reward from them.

I was called in for an interview with a Squadron Leader. He wanted to know which schools I had been educated at, when did I leave school, what work had I done and so forth. Then he smiled at me and told me that he would recommend that I should be promoted to the rank of Warrant Officer. I was immensely gratified and left his office smiling. Then I found that everyone had been recommended for promotion to this rank — except for 10% who had been recommended for a commission. For the first time I realised that the artfulness of RAF officers was boundless. It was 18 months later and after many nasty moments before I reached the promised rank.

In due course the gunnery training started. We had to learn everything it was possible to know about the Browning .303 machine gun and the Boulton Paul gun turret and how they worked. A machine gun is an immensely complicated and efficient piece of equipment. We sat for hours in the classrooms studying the details of the gun and the make-up of the different shells. One day the news went out that the whole gunnery school was to be relocated at another RAF station. A place called 'C.K.' in the wilds of Scotland where it rained all the time and was very cold and there was nothing at all to do. Like everyone else I was downhearted at this sombre news until I found out that we were moving to Castle Kennedy — just a couple of miles away from my home. Great news! One day we embarked on a very long train at Llanfair PG or, in full Llanfairpwllgwyngyllgogerychwrndrobwllantsiliogogoch!

and travelled all day and most of the night, arriving at Castle Kennedy railway station early in the morning. Here I was, not far from home!

## RAF Castle Kennedy      No 3 Air Gunnery School

From the station we were conducted out along the main road and into the camp, the area where the council houses are now. In this area was the domestic site, the cookhouse, the NAAFI, the Gymnasium etc. Our living huts were up on the skyline next to the railway line. The gunnery classrooms were among the trees in Lochinch grounds at the north side of the A75. We soon found our way about. The air gunner's programme recommenced without delay and we started to learn the air gunner's trade. Hours were spent on aircraft recognition and wingspan sizes. Many more hours were taken up with sitting behind a ring-sight watching films of planes appearing out of the distance, identifying them and, if enemy, affecting to shoot them down when they came within range before they could get us. This was not a game. We realised that almost certainly our skills would be needed soon.

Then we had flights to put our skills into practice. We were flown out to sea just off Portpatrick in Anson aircraft and our targets were long drogues, the size of a fighter plane, towed by a Fairey Battle single engined plane. During the first flights we used cameras and cine film. After that we used the Browning machine guns. The planes weaved about so we had to aim carefully to hit the drogue and not the Battle. After each flight the drogues were laid out on the ground so that we could count how many hits we had achieved. I had 4 flights using the camera and 13 flights firing the guns, 2,700 rounds in all. One night we were taken out to what I recognised to be Clayshant Farm where a small model plane had been fitted on to a track laid out in a field facing the sea. Our night fighter training consisted of firing at this model as it ran round the track in the dark. In December 1943, at the end of the course, there was a little ceremony for those who had passed. Out of the 120 entrants I had passed out 13th, so I had the honour of sitting in the front seats with the top twenty. The CO said a few words and then, later that day we received an AG brevet and sergeant stripes. When I got home that night, I surprised my mother by giving her the brevet and stripes to sew on to my uniform. I now had the rank of sergeant with three stripes on my arm and a Sparks badge and an air gunner's brevet. What a proud chap I was! Also my pay was increased to 9/- a day. My father and mother congratulated me. I then had 14 days leave at home and was posted to Hooton Park, No.11 Radio School, an RAF station half way between Liverpool and Chester; arriving there on 22nd December, 1943. I think that it is now the site of the large Vauxhall motor car factory at Ellesmere Port.

## Radar Course, RAF Hooton Park

I spent Christmas at Hooton Park. The Christmas lunch was, as tradition dictates, served to us by the officers, and was very good. At the course there, we learned about Air to Sea Radar: this was a new thing and very secret. We were instructed that on no account were we to say anything about what we were doing and we were told not to try to understand how the radar worked in case we were captured and gave away information. All we knew was how to switch on the radar set and look at the screen and interpret the information it gave. I had a number of flights, one in a Blackburn Botha and five in 'Faithful Annies' totalling 10.40 hours. We flew out over the Irish Sea to pick up 'blips' on the radar screen and see what they were. Usually a 'blip' turned out to be a ship, but on one occasion I identified a Martello Tower as a ship! Practice makes perfection and soon I could pick out ships over 30 miles away and even make a guess at their size. We had a lot of walking about to do. Our party of twenty sergeants lived in a large country mansion house about a mile from the domestic site. At one time Hooton Park had been a country estate and possibly our house had been the big house, Hooton Hall.

Our training course there was completed in February 1944. We were now ready to go to an operational squadron. It had taken seventeen months. We were posted back to Blackpool to join the aircrew pool, ready to be sent to a squadron. I was 20 years old.

During the months of training at the different camps we were always wakened at 06.30 to walk to the ablution block to wash and shave then walk to the cookhouse for breakfast and be on the parade ground for eight o'clock, ready to start the working day. As well as training for the job we were also kept very fit: we always had a couple of hours in the gym every week when we did PT, boxing and wrestling and running. Some camps had ropes stretched out high up between trees and we would have to carry out Tarzan-like manoeuvres clambering along the ropes. On Wednesday afternoons we were sent out to play football. On Sundays there was sometimes a Church Parade. We would be marched to a church where we would sit in ignorant silence thinking of how we would spend the rest of the day when we were released. In some camps the food had been very good indeed; in others it was awful. RAF discipline was strict, but I don't remember anyone being bullied by the NCOs. The best thing was the sense of comradeship: one always had pals to go about with.

## Aircrew Pool, Blackpool

In the pool there was not very much to do. We had to be on parade at 8 o'clock and then they would give us lectures or PT or find something to keep us occupied or even just let us clear off. Some of us used to meet in a café at 10.15 for coffee and a cake and see who could be the first to complete the Daily Express crossword. I had taken up ice skating, so I would slip away to the Pleasure Beach every time I got the chance to practise skating. I could not dance so decided to learn and started to attend a dance class. It was great being in Blackpool with not a lot do except enjoy myself.

At Blackpool I was in a billet in 5 Lord Street near the Central

*The sergeants with their landlady at Lord Street, Blackpool.
The author standing second from left.*

Station with a number of other air-crew sergeants. The landlady was a good sort with a heart of gold who fed us very well.

It was now early 1944 and Bomber Command aircraft were making huge attacks nearly every night on enemy targets in Germany and north-west Europe. Because we wore an aircrew brevet and sergeant's stripes, people looked upon us also as men of exceptional courage and daring, to be celebrated for our exploits. We were enjoying the reflected glory of other men's heroism. Then one day when listening to the BBC News on the wireless about the previous night's raid we heard that 81 planes had failed to return: I realised that with seven men in each plane more than 550 men had failed to return, many of them killed. It was Bomber Command policy at the time that a 'tour' on bomber operations was thirty sorties over Germany so the arithmetic was not good! At losses of about 8% every night then in theory there was very little chance of getting through a tour. I worried a bit. How long would we have before we were sent to a squadron? I started to wonder how I would die. Never mind! Cheer up! I might be lucky!

# Troopship — Destination Unknown

There were hundreds of aircrew in Blackpool all waiting to go to squadrons. Then, in April 1944 the news came through that we were being posted abroad. We didn't know where we were going, or whether it was a good thing. We were issued with tropical uniforms, even a pith helmet, and then given fourteen days embarkation leave. I spent a lot of my time at home making a new large kennel for our black and white collie dog, Gyp. I got it finished in time and he liked his new den very much. When the leave was up, my father took me to Stranraer harbour station in his Austin 12 car with my three kitbags—one RAF uniform, one flying kit and one overseas kit. It was almost too heavy to carry it all. My father became a bit emotional, thinking that he might lose a son.

At Blackpool it wasn't long before we were entrained to an 'unknown destination'. This turned out to be Liverpool docks where we embarked on board the *SS Orion* troopship. The ship left harbour and turned north up the Irish Sea where we were joined by other ships to make up a large convoy attended by small warships. After passing the familiar coastline at the mouth of Lochryan and travelling farther north, we then turned left and for two days steamed west. How wonderful, we thought: we are going to America, but no, we weren't. We turned south for a couple of days then east through the Straits of Gibraltar into the Mediterranean and right along it to Port Said in Egypt.

The journey in the troopship was a nightmare. It was said that there were 10,000 airmen on board, all but a few being aircrew sergeants. We lived on mess-decks with 20 at a table, and 2 'volunteers' armed with enamelled pails were sent to queue up for buckets of mush for us to eat off our tin plates. There was so little in the pails that we were always hungry and ready to eat anything that was offered. At night, the tables were folded away and hammocks slung up on hooks in the ceilings. They were so close together that one could hardly move.

There was worse to come: with others we were 'volunteered' to man the Oerlikon anti-aircraft guns. There were about twelve guns, each fitted into emplacements built up high at the sides of the ship. A pal and I had to man one of these guns on 'Ship's Bell' rotas of two, four or eight hour shifts. It was terribly cold and wet, standing out exposed in the middle of the freezing Atlantic gales in April. We wore all our clothes and an overcoat, duffle coat with hood and waterproof ground sheet and southwester hat and still we were wet, frozen and dejected. To add to our woes, if we were on watch when the buckets of food arrived, the others ate everything among them and kept nothing for those on duty. Also, as we were not allowed to sling our hammocks during the day and there was no room at night, there was no provision for catching up on sleep. We tried to sleep standing up against a wall in a small cupboard, without much success. Then we found a staircase that led down to a dark empty place near the keel where we discovered hooks and could hang hammocks and have a few hours of sleep undisturbed except for the creaking of the ship and the sounds of small sinister scratching and rustlings. When we entered the Mediterranean, the weather changed, the sun shone, and it was a different world. From our eyrie in the gun turret we could see the 'upper class', those with rings on their sleeves rather than common stripes, walking the decks, and appearing in their smart made-to-measure tropical outfits. There even were a few WAAFs knocking about. Apart from starving, the last few days were pleasant enough and eventually we docked at Port Said feeling glad to be off the ship.

## Egypt and the Holy Land

The Transit Camp in Port Said was a tented camp with few facilities. We had to put down our groundsheets and sleep on the sand. After a week we were posted somewhere else. We found ourselves entrained, being taken north up to Gaza and then Jerusalem. I was in Jerusalem for six weeks living in what had been the German Embassy. We were just waiting to move to a squadron, so there was little to do except to sightsee. I joined a group, meeting at St. Andrew's church, where two or three times a week we visited places with biblical connections and listened to talks. We entered the Church of the Holy Sepulchre and spent some time at the Wailing Wall watching the Jews making their devotions. The Old City was mainly a bazaar with skilled Arab people making things to sell. It was quite dirty and smelly and the food stalls were covered with flies. One day I set off early on one of the local buses to Tel Aviv. It was a slow journey along a poor road, stopping and starting at the Arab villages and allowing me to see how the Arabs lived. These were the days of the Stern Gang, fighting for a Jewish national home and, if anything, we were on the side of the Arabs who were so poor. When the bus arrived eventually at Tel Aviv, I was able to walk around this large, modern city on the coast and admire the buildings and shops. Jaffa, a mile or two along the sea front, was a bustling port full of small ships. I walked back to Tel Aviv and took the bus back to Jerusalem pleased with my visit.

My next posting was to RAF Gianaclis, a large RAF station near Cairo in Egypt. I went into Cairo with some of the other men and took the opportunity to travel out by tram to see the Pyramids and the Sphinx. Four of us climbed up the huge stone blocks until we were half way up the largest Pyramid and then took some photographs.

Sometime in June at Gianaclis, 100 of us were ushered into a large tent, asked to split into groups of ten and move to one of the tables. At our table we were sworn into the South African Air Force and welcomed into 22 South African Squadron with the information that we would be moving immediately to Gibraltar. The other groups were sent to other SAAF squadrons. We were quite pleased and excited to be part of the South African Air Force. A few days later we were taken out to Cairo West RAF station and were flown to Gibraltar. As we passed over El Alamein, we saw the remains of the battle, the tanks and guns still strewn all over the desert sands. The Dakota plane had limited endurance so we had to come down often to refuel. We landed at Marble Arch and Castle Benito for fuel and food and stayed for a night at Biskra, a small Arab town with a landing strip. From Biskra we were flown on to Algiers where we refuelled and then crossed over the Med to land at Gibraltar, arriving in the afternoon of 9th July 1944. The ten of us were taken to a Nissen hut at the side of the runway where we each took over a bed and dumped our kit bags. That hut was to be our home for the next twelve months until July 1945.

## Sgt. Fidler goes to War

Gibraltar is a huge limestone rock, 1,300 feet high and is linked to Spain by a narrow isthmus of flat land that was used mainly as the RAF station North Front. In 1942 the runway had been extended out into Gibraltar Bay, making the runway double the length and useable by the largest planes of that time. To get into Gibraltar town we had to cross the runway when it was clear and walk into Main Street, where all the shops and pubs and places of interest were. It was not a very interesting town. The Gibraltarians were severely rationed. One could have a cup of coffee in the café but it would have powdered milk and saccharine sweetener and there was nothing at all to eat. We could only go so far along the front and not very far into the harbour or up the road leading to the Army fortifications.

# No 22 Squadron, South African Air Force

In front of our huts were the ten planes being operated by 22 Squadron, the very ones that we were to fly in over the coming months. These were American Lockheed Ventura PV1s. They had two Pratt and Whitney radial engines each developing 1,800 h.p. The take off speed was 90 knots and the cruising speed was 180 knots. They carried a bomb load of 10 depth charges and had two supplementary long range fuel tanks under the wings giving an endurance of 6-7 hours. The armaments were two forward-firing fixed guns in the nose, a Martin upper mid turret holding two .50in. machine guns and two .300 in a ventral tunnel firing backwards and downwards. The wireless receiver and transmitter was a Bendix model and the radar was the latest air-to-sea model. The crew comprised one pilot, one navigator and three wireless operator/air gunner/radar operators. The reason we were taken on was because the aircraft had only four of a crew and needed one each of us to make the crews up to five. All the SAAF aircrew were officers, so we thought we would be commissioned, but this was not to be; we remained as sergeants for most of the time we were with them. Since we were overseas we now were paid 12/- a day.

We had a talk in the Ops room from an intelligence officer who explained to us that our job would be to fly out to the area in the Atlantic where U-Boats were believed to be, to find them and attack them, escort the convoys coming down from Britain and, very importantly, make sure that no U-Boats slipped through the Straits of Gibraltar into the Mediterranean. If even one U-Boat entered the Med, then all of the ships in Mediterranean waters would be in danger. Then he took us up to the roof of the building and pointed out a lookout post just a short distance across the border into Spain where the Spaniards watched all the aircraft movements and had a direct line to Berlin to report everything we did. The squadron CO was Lt. Col. Rademann and the two flight commanders were Major

*American Lockheed Ventura PV1*

Catchpole and Major Wood. My first flight with 22 Squadron was on 24th July 1944 when I flew with Major Wood as a passenger on a bombing exercise.

Shortly afterwards the aircrew were made up into crews. The crew that I was in was as follows:

| | | |
|---|---|---|
| Captain Hadley Golding | SAAF | Pilot |
| Lieutenant Gordon Cummings. | SAAF | Navigator |
| Lieutenant (?) Roberts | SAAF | Wireless Op/ Gunner/ Radar Op. |
| Warrant Officer Bob Sumner | SAAF | " " |
| Sergeant Norman Fidler | RAF | " " |

When we first met as a crew, Capt. Golding, who came from Capetown and was 28 years old, showed us lovely photographs of himself and wife and son and daughter. He continued that although he intended to do a good job, he wanted to get home again safely to his family and if anyone in his crew could not do their work properly he would put him under close arrest. Later I discovered that all the pilots had been instructed to deliver the same threat to their crews. Gordon Cummings had been a barrister in Durban. He was a good pianist, could speak French well, could take shorthand and was a very good all rounder. Roberts came from Johannesburg and had been a mine captain in the gold mines. Bob Sumner came from Liverpool and had been in the Palestine Police for three years before volunteering for the SAAF.

Our first few trips were exercises with a British submarine stationed in Gibraltar. The submarine would make its way into the Med and submerge, showing on the surface only a representation of a snorkel for us to search for, using the radar. When found, the pilot flew over the track of the supposed enemy, dropping a string of smoke floats. This was a very interesting pastime, giving us a very good idea of what we would be looking for in the future. We also got a trip in the submarine round the Rock and into the Med where we dived and experienced life in a sub for a few hours.

*Captain Hadley Golding and crew.
Author standing on left.*

After a few weeks of exercises for the crew to become accustomed to the planes and to flying off Gibraltar, on 26th August 1944 we flew on our first operational mission, called a U-boat operational sweep, a flight of 4 hours 30min, out into the Atlantic. For the next eight months until VE Day we went out into the Atlantic, usually every third day, on anti-U-boat patrols or convoy escort duty or air-sea rescue search if a plane had 'failed to return'.

The best task was that of convoy escort. It was an impressive sight to see a large number of merchant ships steaming along in convoy with corvettes and destroyers guarding them. On arrival we had to signal by Aldis lamp to the largest warship to request instructions and usually the reply was for us to search the area a mile in front. I liked to think that our presence overhead was useful in deterring any submarine commander who thought of attacking the convoy. As we flew over the Straits we could usually see a group of corvettes searching for echoes of submarines on their Asdic equipment. Many of the flights were quite boring. My main function was to sit in the nose of the plane at the radar and search for a 'blip' which might indicate a snorkel or a submarine. This job was shared with Bob. Roberts would bag the WOP seat. What he had to do was to listen out on the radio on the hour to find out if there was a message for us. I was the one who fired the guns. Very often on the journey out to our patrol area, the skipper would tell me to drop a smoke float then I would go up to the gun turret and, as the plane circled, fire a few bursts of .5 ammunition at the float, for practice. The crew seemed to enjoy looking out to see the results of my firing: sometimes I fired the little .300in guns. We never used the two forward-firing guns.

If anything went wrong with the wireless or the radar or the guns, then I was always the one asked to find out the reason and take responsibility if we had to return to base. In my opinion the SAAF men had not the same expertise as the RAF aircrew.

On every flight, a box containing sweets and bars of chocolate was put on board for us to eat. To my chagrin, the skipper ordered that the box should not be opened and should be left in the plane for the ground staff, in the belief that they would give superior attention to us and our aircraft. After each flight the crew would hasten to a special aircrew cookhouse to have a great fry-up of bacon and eggs etc. with the treat of real butter, milk and sugar on the table. We could eat as much as we wanted, so we made the most of it as the food in the sergeants' mess was very poor being mostly bully beef turned out in different ways. The South African men in our crew decided that as their food in the officers' mess was excellent, they did not need the after flight meal so they didn't join us.

As all of the SAAF air crew were commissioned except Bob Sumner we really did not have much opportunity to mix with them except when flying. The exception was a couple of times when a crowd of them came down to our hut with bottles and we had a party and a sing-song and jokes. We sang 'Take me back to the old

*Our British sub off Gibraltar.*

Transvaal', 'Capetown, it is the place for me' and other South African songs. Then someone would sing 'The old red flannel drawers that Maggie wore' and the party would go downhill after that.

Also based in Gibraltar was 455 New Zealand Squadron whose CO was Wing Comm. James. They flew in Wellingtons fitted with Leigh Lights (searchlights to light up any submarine detected at night) and of course they carried out the night patrols on anti-submarine searches while we flew during the day. There was also a squadron of flying boats, Sunderlands and Catalinas, in Gibraltar harbour. Sometimes in calm weather we would see an American blimp from Port Lyoutey down the Moroccan coast patrolling the straits.

## Mishaps

There were a number of unusual events. One afternoon an American Dakota landed, to be followed a minute later by another, then another and another and another until the aerodrome was covered by 100 Dakotas parked at one side of the runway. In the morning they set off again flying east. We realised that they were going to Italy. The planes arrived back a few weeks later but we saw only 92 this time. The crews told us that they had participated in parachute drops in Italy where there was furious fighting.

Sometimes one of our Venturas 'Failed to Return' which was always a sad occasion. A couple of planes would be sent out to look for wreckage but we never saw anything. We lost five crews, 25 men.

One day one of our Venturas was unable to stop when landing and went off the west end of the runway, into the sea. The crew managed to get out safely but the plane was a write-off. The pilot claimed that the brakes had failed. A flight commander ticked off the erring pilot, reminding him that there was an emergency braking system that could have been used. The pilot said he thought the emergency system was unworkable in the circumstances. He was

*Some SAAF personnel in front of a Ventura with the Rock in the background.*

told it was perfectly simple. All you had to do was to run to the end of the runway, pull up a lever that locked one of the wheels, the plane would then spin round and when it faced the opposite way, the lever should be released and the plane would run back down the runway until it stopped. He then announced that he would give a demonstration the next day. Everyone thought he was very courageous, except his crew who would have to fly with him. They said it was a rash and very dangerous project and urged him to think again, however the pilot looked forward to showing everyone what he could do and could not be dissuaded.

The next morning , the plane took off and flew round the other side of the Rock and appeared over the bay of Gibraltar ready to touch down on the west end of the runway which jutted out into the sea. The pilot intended to run down to the wider end, approach close to the side of a large brick wall surrounding the 'graveyard' where remains of crashed planes were dumped, and turn round there and run back again. I was not flying that morning so was able to join the crowd of onlookers anxious to see this amazing feat. The plane touched down and bounced up as usual, then after some small bounces, ran smoothly along the tarmac rushing past us at speed until it reached the side of the brick wall when there was a loud screech from the wheels and the plane turned.

Something had gone wrong, however: the plane turned the wrong way. There had been a miscalculation. Instead of turning right, onto the other side of the runway where there was plenty of room, it turned left going headfirst into the brick wall. We saw the nose crumple up like an eggshell and the two engines bury themselves into the wall before the plane stopped. The fire engines raced down the runway but the plane did not catch fire. The aircrew were extricated from the wreckage and taken to the Medical Room but were not hurt. Although the scheme had not come off and a plane had been lost, the flight commander's reputation for bravery had been enhanced. It was a story that was retold many times — and those who were not there were sorry to have missed it.

I had some difficulty with my armament mechanic. I liked to

practice and test the .5s every time we flew, so he had to clean the guns on our plane, S for Sugar, after every flight. It was not a big job but he complained about this saying that no one else had to clean their guns so often and he became quite bitter to the extent of sometimes 'fixing' the guns so that they would not fire. I took him aside and threatened him with 'jankers' if he re-offended. However, he made the guns unserviceable once again, so the skipper promptly returned to base and called out the Major who then put the mechanic in the Guardroom under close arrest. I don't know what punishment he received because I never saw or heard of him again. I was given a different armourer who was very satisfactory and anxious to please, but the rest of the ground staff became very sulky and bolshy.

The next time we flew, I noticed that the dial indicating the amount of power from the generator to the battery was showing nil. I discussed this unusual matter with the skipper as I thought that possibly the battery was not being charged. He ordered that the wireless and the radar should be switched off to conserve power and we returned to base in worried silence. We got back alright and I had

*22 Squadron at the Rock. Note the extra fuel tanks which were fixed under the wings.*

to face up to the Major who did not agree with my assessment. He claimed that the battery would be fully charged and that I had made a mistake and that we should get into the plane and fly it. I said that I did not want to fly in it. Fortunately the skipper agreed with me and demanded another plane. The Major was extremely angry, but he gave us 'Y' for Yankee to use and off we went to complete our task which we did without any more ado. We got back alright, had a meal and got to bed.

In the middle of the night we were awakened to go on Air Sea Rescue. One of our planes had not come back and we were to go out over the area and search for wreckage. Which plane was it I asked? 'S for Sugar' I was informed. In my opinion, they must have sent out the plane without having it checked over and the plane and a crew of five were lost.

## Neutral Spanish ship *Ciudad de Sevilla*

There was a neutral Spanish ship called *Ciudad de Sevilla* that plied between South America and Cadiz, just to the west of Gibraltar, and as it was suspected of carrying contraband, one of our planes always had to meet it and make it call in to Gibraltar to be searched. On one occasion our navigator, Gordon Cummings, was convinced that the ship was aiming for Cadiz instead of where we wanted. I was told to send an Aldis message 'Gibraltar'. Still Gordon was not happy. The skipper called me over. I was to fire into the sea in front of the ship. He would fly above the bow of the ship and I would fire forward into the sea. The task had to be carried out carefully because the ship was neutral. The job was simple enough and I fired without endangering the ship at all. As I came down out of the turret I could see that the ship had stopped and was wallowing in the waves. Then a great line of flags was run up. I got out the book and started to read the flags but in no time they were pulled down and a new lot of flags was run up. No-one understood what was happening, but eventually the ship was underway again and Gordon was happy with the course it was on which took it into Gibraltar.

One of the SAAF pilots was the worst pilot ever known. No-one would fly with him. I won't give his name just in case he is still about. Anytime some unfortunate was ordered to take him out for circuits and bumps, the whole squadron would take out chairs and forms and go out to the edge of the runway to see the event. His approach was always too fast and high and he would flop down from a height with a crunch, and bounce up and down again but always managed to stop at the end of the runway somehow. He should have been given another job and not have been allowed to fly.

In the winter 1944/45 it became freezing cold and very draughty in the planes. Suddenly all the SAAF aircrew started to appear in leather bomber jackets which they had lend-leased from the Americans. They had their photographs taken looking like the film star Errol Flynn. I requested a jacket too but the answer was "No, we should use our RAF flying overalls. No-one had thought of that. I became the guinea pig and on getting out the inner and outer suit tried on the inner suit. It was a brown colour and was puffed out with a kapok filling. It was lovely, warm and cosy even outside in the winter wind, but I looked like the Michelin Man or a big brown bear and I had to stand some jocularity. The next time I flew I carried my inner suit and placed it in the back of the plane. After take-off, I donned my outfit together with a balaclava helmet and walked forward and sat next to the pilot and looked forward nonchalantly. Captain Golding just about had a fit when he saw me. After he had recovered from the shock he wanted to know what I was playing at. I explained that the rest of the crew had their warm bomber jackets so I was wearing my RAF flying suit and that I would be wearing it in future during the cold days of winter. He wasn't happy. I wore the suit the next time we flew but then abandoned it. None of the other RAF sergeants wore their flying suits either.

There were ten of us RAF sergeant WOP/AGs in one of the black Nissen huts near the side of the runway at Gibraltar. Between us and the runway were parked about a dozen Corsair single engined planes that had come from a large aircraft carrier being repaired in Gibraltar harbour. A few yards away at the back of the huts was the high barbed wire fence marking the Spanish frontier. A couple of hundred yards to the east was the end of the runway and the sandy beach where, off duty, in the summer, we could lie about and sunbathe or swim in the sea.

*Neutral Spanish ship Ciudad de Sevilla*

*Our home-made bathing raft.*

We made a raft out of empty oil cans and spare planks of wood and paddled it around. As well as myself there was Bill Boddington, Robert Proudley, Cyril Holdridge, Kenneth Stuart (Paddy) Riley, 'Tyke' Davies, 'Ossey' Thornlea, A. Chevington, 'Joe' King and one other whose name I have forgotten but whose face I can remember. We all, except Chevington, who was posted to Italy a few weeks after arriving, lived in that hut from 9th July 1944 until July 1945.

'Paddy' Riley was lost with his crew in a plane that 'Failed to Return' just a few days before Christmas 1944. In Paddy's crew were Lt. J.W.M. Treu (pilot), Lt. W. H. Taylor, Lt K.E. Ribbink, and F./S. James Scott Hogg. Scottie lived in the hut next door to ours. By a remarkable coincidence his father was the postmaster at Ardwell near Stranraer and Scottie's name is included on the war memorial at Ardwell Church. Paddy's mother was a widow and lived at 9 Monkbridge Ave, Leeds 6, just a few doors away from my uncle's house. During the war there was nothing at the time to mark someone's death, but Paddy, who was always cheerful and lively and full of jokes, was missed greatly and we all mourned him very much. He was a great chap. Hogg's and Riley's names and all the other 22 Squadron aircrew lost flying from Gibraltar are listed on the Malta Memorial. The Malta Memorial, built on a site generously provided by the Government of Malta, commemorates those who lost their lives whilst serving with the Commonwealth Air Forces flying from bases in the Mediterranean area and have no known grave. When on holiday in Malta in 2003 I saw the memorial and picked out the names of many of the men I had known all that time ago.

22 Squadron also had a tented camp at La Senia, the American Air Force base not far from Oran in Algeria. Our planes were flown there to take advantage of the facilities, spare parts and replacement engines available to service these American-built planes. Every so often we would have two or three days there which made a change for us. The South Africans had a squad there who did all the dirty work, like cleaning the latrines, etc. I felt that they were treated very poorly and roughly, but when I protested I was told that I should not worry. It was alright for us, I was told, but the whites in Africa had to live with them.

Once, some of us were offered a visit to Sidi Bel Abbes, the home of the French Foreign Legion, about 30 or 40 miles away. It was a very uncomfortable journey along a poor, untarred, lonely road, hanging on inside the back of a lorry. I had been told to take my Smith and Wesson revolver for protection and because of the poor Arab habitations we passed through, I was glad we could defend ourselves if necessary. When we finally arrived at our destination, the officers were welcomed into the headquarters for hospitality — and the rest of us looked round the township. I had my camera which meant that I was able to take some good photographs of the barracks and headquarters. We had tins of cigarettes for barter and tried to find something to eat but without avail, so we had to stay hungry. There was a great food shortage in Morocco and Algeria at that time during the war, the only places open were the estaminets, so we all trooped into these bars and drank wine and liquors. An amusing side of our visit was that we were trailed by a group of street walkers who followed us round and had to be ordered out all the time. One member of our party soon became maudlin and affectionate with one of the women, saying he was going to stay with her and not return to the squadron. What a job we had, carrying him back to the truck against his will and flinging him on board! Then the officers returned in a very 'happy mood' and we got back to the camp eventually.

From La Senia we could walk to a small village called Valmy where there was a little bar favoured by the 22 Squadron airmen. All we could have there was wine, but it was a good meeting place and the daughter Didi Valour and her mother were nice people who made us feel at home. Bob Sumner and I used to go into Oran, which was a large, interesting town with modern buildings in the French style and nice seafront and also a Kasbah in the centre — the Arab poor part of the town where it was unsafe to venture. There were also American canteens where we could have very good food and buy sweets and chocolate. As well as Oran, we sometimes had occasion to fly for an overnight visit to Algiers on the Mediterranean coast and Port Lyoutey, Casablanca and Rabat, all on the North African, Moroccan coast. These were all pleasant, French/Arab places to visit and made a great change from the dullness of Gibraltar.

*Page of my flying log book entries for November 1944*
*(lighter print, which would have been in red, denotes night flying)*

# The D Day Invasion of Normandy on 6th June 1944

The D Day landings of June 1944 occurred while we were at Gib. When we heard on the wireless the great news, we were all elated. In some ways we were disappointed that there was no part for us to play but at the same time we thought we were lucky to be in a comparatively safe place. If we were needed we were always there to be called upon. Meanwhile we carried on with our anti-submarine patrols and convoy escorts. We could follow the progress of the war by listening to the BBC news bulletin and by reading the *Gibraltar Chronicle*, the local newspaper.

# VE Day

Eventually the Germans were beaten and they surrendered, culminating in VE Day on 8th May 1945. What a wonderful time that was. It was almost unbelievable that the war was over and that we had won and that before long we would be on our way home. We celebrated by having parties in the sergeants' mess and shaking hands with one another and some people becoming a bit too much under the weather. The CO decided to celebrate everything by flying a formation round the Rock. It was foolhardy to take off in V formation on such a narrow runway, and I was glad that we were allowed to land separately.

Then we heard that the U-boats in the area had been instructed to go to certain positions at a particular time and surface and show a white flag and surrender to our warships. The CO was the first to go out and our plane was the second. Looking out on the radar I could see a conglomeration of blips in the area and then as we approached I left the radar set for the last time and looked out of the gun turret to see no less than three large, black, evil-looking U-Boats, all showing white flags with a number of corvettes taking charge of them. The CO's and our plane circled round the boats, just looking at what was going on, for the extent of our endurance until another of our planes arrived to take over. A few days later I saw in the *Gibraltar Chronicle* a report of the surrender with a picture of our plane circling the submarines and ships. The CO had taken one of the squadron's photographers in his plane to take mementos of the day's events. I still have a copy of that newspaper.

The U-boat crews were held in a compound down at the harbour. The compound was surrounded by a wire fence. We could see the Germans walking about inside. We had been told that on arrival in Gibraltar they had been cowed and frightened but on finding that they were to be treated fairly they became insolent saying that they had seen our planes flying about but we couldn't find them. The rumour went about that Lt. Col. Rademann asked the authorities for permission to take a party of us (including me), to pick a fight with them and beat them up. I looked forward to the visit and wondered how we would fare. However the visit did not take place.

On 26th May 1945 I was in a party of 22 squadron's RAF sergeants taken to Rabat for a fortnight's leave. We were billeted in a large house on the Atlantic coast. We enjoyed proper food, could swim in the sea in the little bay in front of the house and could travel into Rabat, a short distance into the town. It was a very pleasant, relaxing holiday. We returned to Gibraltar thinking that maybe we would be posted back to Britain.

Back in Gibraltar we were not given anything to do. We spent our time lazing on the beach or going into town. The news came that the squadron had been awarded two DFCs and one DFM. The CO and his navigator received the DFCs. The DFM was for an NCO so we wondered if one of us would receive it. However it was granted to the sergeant pay clerk. None of us expected to be given it, so no one was disappointed.

Then we were told that we were to leave the squadron and move to an RAF station in Algiers. We had the usual drinks party and shook hands etc. and then on the 19th June 1945 we were flown to a small tented camp on the Mediterranean coast a couple of miles east of Algiers. There must have been about 20 of us. It was very nice being there; the food was super, the best I had received in the RAF, nothing much to do though except to lounge about on the beach or go into Algiers but there was no aerodrome on the camp and I could not see why we were there. I wondered if something wonderful like being sent home was in store for us or if it was something terrible like being posted out to Burma. Then eventually we were told. We were sent back to Gibraltar to rejoin 22 Squadron. We got back into the same hut, the same nine of us and in the same crews and in a week or two we were told that the squadron was moving back to the Middle East. We thought that we were being despatched to the Far East to take part in the war there.

## Back to the Middle East

The South African aircrew flew the planes and the RAF aircrew travelled by ship across the Mediterranean on the *SS Bergansfjord*. We had a comfortable journey in cabins and excellent food. When we arrived at Port Said, we were transferred to RAF station Gianaclis where we met up with the rest of 22 Squadron. While I was at Gianaclis the atom bombs were dropped on Hiroshima and Nagasaki, ending the war with Japan. On VJ Day, 15th August 1945, there was a celebration in the camp with a special lunch and a sports event. Everyone was very happy and in an exuberant mood and thought that soon we would be on the boat home. It was a wonderful day! In the afternoon I went into Cairo to see if there was anything special on, but apart from the bars and dives doing a roaring trade, there was nothing to see. From Gianaclis the squadron moved to RAF Idcu, a small aerodrome about ten miles from Alexandria. Then some of the crews, including my crew, were sent back to South Africa so I said goodbye to them and never saw any of them again.

A week later when looking at the flying roster, I was dumfounded to see that I was down to fly with the pilot I have previously described as 'the worst pilot ever known'. I noticed that there were two other RAF flight sergeants down to fly with him but no SAAF people. We three RAF realised that we were being the mugs and were resentful, but in the services one just had to do what one was told. The next day when we met the pilot he had the nerve to give us the 'close arrest' talk. We soon realised that he was just the same hopeless pilot and that our lives were at risk all the time we flew with him. From the air we saw crowds of onlookers appearing down below to watch his circuits and bumps and his 'hairy' landings. It was terrible to be in the plane when he crashed down; the whole plane shuddered. We thought the undercarriage would break every time we landed. We had to fly with him seven times from 4th August to 29th September 1945. Then the next day when in the sergeants' mess, I saw someone put up a notice asking for a volunteer to act as a ground wireless operator! I put my name down immediately, right at the top of the page, and the following morning went into the orderly room and got the post. What a relief. No more flying with the duffer!

My new job was quite a humble but useful one which helped to keep all the stations in Egypt in touch with one another by landline. The news came that 22 Squadron was to move back to South Africa, but the RAF aircrew was to stay in the Middle East. I was posted to Aden and the others were posted to other RAF stations. I was sorry to leave my pals with whom I had flown for so long and had shared tribulations — and successes. I think we could call ourselves a Band of Brothers. I often think of them all and can still see their faces, although I suppose that many of them will have passed on by now. On 24th October 1945 I was taken to RAF Cairo West with about a dozen other aircrew and in a Dakota piloted by a F/Lt. Coates we were flown to RAF Khormaksar in Aden, landing on the way at Wadi Halfa, Khartoum, and Asmara to drop off and pick up other personnel.

## Flying from Khormaksar in Aden

At Khormaksar I found I was on the Communications Flight. It had a number of planes, Vickers Wellingtons, Lockheed PV1 Venturas, Fairey Albacores, Martin Baltimores and others. The armaments and gun turrets had been removed from the planes. Aden was at the centre of a huge area with many small RAF stations and landing places all along the coast and inland and our job was to deliver supplies and personnel to all of these places. There also were commitments to places in Eritrea which meant flying over the Red Sea to the African coast. My first flight was on 28th October, 1945, in a Ventura flown by a F/Lt. Tylman to Ryan, an RAF station about 150 miles down the coast and then back again the next day. I found that I had to fly in any plane and was expected to know how to operate the wireless set and direction finder, so I had to relearn the British sets that I had not used since training days. The second flight was in an Albacore. I got to the plane in good time and saw the mechanics push it out of the hangar and then push back the wings to secure them (the Albacores were biplanes that had been used on aircraft carriers and had folding wings).We were to take a native soldier to an inland village called Beihan. It took us 1 hr 20mins to get there so it was about a hundred miles away.

***Fairey Albacore biplane***

When we got to the village I could not see a runway but there were crowds of white clad figures bending down to pick up stones. The pilot landed in the area on the sand that had been cleared of stones. The District Officer arrived, a grand figure riding a fine white horse, and he took us into his dwelling where we sat on the floor and his servant served us with little cups of green tea. (Tip — if you are ever offered green tea, say that you are not thirsty). We then took another soldier into the plane and returned to Aden. During the three months that I was stationed at Aden I had 34 flights, many in Venturas and Albacores, and one in a Wellington and one in a Baltimore.

*Some RAF personnel standing beside an Albacore at an Arab village.*

It was quite interesting because one never knew until first thing in the morning what one was flying in, with whom and where to. We had to arrive at the Duty Room at 6.30am, find out what was on, go for breakfast and back to the Duty Room ready to fly. Aden is one of the hottest places in the world so we liked to set off early before the plane became baking hot.

When we had to stay overnight, at the most outlying places we would have a film with us to give some entertainment to the personnel there. A screen would be erected and a film shown, usually a Bob Hope comedy. We would sit at one side of the screen and the Arabs at the other.

There was always great competition by crew members to fly with the most reliable pilots. On one flight in a Ventura the pilot was a WO Jones. I noticed that he carried out his before-flight routine very carefully and his landings and take offs were excellent so I told him that I was experienced with Venturas having been on a Ventura squadron for a year and would like to fly with him when possible. He was quite pleased and agreed to put my name up to fly with him. I found that he was studying to go into the ministry and the padre was helping him. He went with the padre every Sunday to play the organ and take some part in the services and sometimes I went with them. Jones told me that he had agreed to become the Chairman of the Sergeants' Mess Committee and that he would like me to be the Treasurer. There wasn't much work in it, he said, so I did the job. I had to collect the messing fees, pay some people, keep an eye on the bar-keeper and the stock, make sure that we made the proper amount of money out of the bar and go to the NAAFI stores every week to buy drink. Then at a Sergeants' Mess meeting I found that it was also my job to run the dance. All I had to do was to tell the cook to put on the same buffet as last time and employ a dance band. The difficulty lay in persuading the few females there were in Aden to come to the dance, to come on their own and not to bring a boy friend with them. The dance went very well, with the help of those who had assisted at previous dances and I got a vote of thanks at the next meeting. While at Aden I was promoted to the rank of Warrant Officer with the pay of 16 shillings a day which meant that I was quite well off.

    Life at Khormaksar was very good. I was given one of the married quarters for myself. It had a veranda, bedroom, kitchen, bathroom and a little yard/garden. The bedroom had two beds, a desk and a large ceiling fan. Also I had a share of an Arab servant who brought a cup of tea in the morning and cleaned my shoes and swept out the place. The food in the Sergeants' Mess was great. We were served by native servants who wore white robes. Although we had to start very early in the morning we finished at 'tiffin' (lunch time). It was extremely hot by noon so we had to lie down in the afternoon and take a siesta. I used to go down to the gym in the evening where a PT sergeant coached weight-lifting and boxing. I became proficient at boxing and entered many between-units contests. On Sunday afternoons the sergeant also arranged for three or four taxis to take the aircrew NCOs out to a sandy bay where we had a picnic and then went into Steamer Point for tea. Steamer Point and Crater were the two towns in Aden.

In early 1946 I was told that I was to be posted home and demobbed early, on compassionate grounds because my father was not keeping well and I was needed to run the business. I liked where I was but I was very pleased to be going home anyway. With all my kit I was flown to Egypt in a Dakota and taken to an RAF station, 22 PTC, just outside Cairo where I had to stay for two or three weeks until my transport was arranged. I then had to take charge of ten RAF personnel who were also going home to be demobbed. We went by train to Port Said and embarked on a troopship which set off to cross the Mediterranean. I was given a cabin and was fed like a lord but my men had to suffer the usual troopship treatment. When we arrived at Toulon we were entrained and for hours travelled through the French countryside until we reached Boulogne. From there we crossed the Channel to Folkestone and took the train to London. Eventually I arrived with my squad of airmen at RAF Uxbridge where I went through the demobilising procedure and selected my demob suit. It would be about March 1946. Then it was off to Euston Station and on to the LMS 'Paddy' line train until I arrived back home at Stranraer at six o'clock in the morning.

The family and the dog were pleased to see me. We had breakfast and I told them about the exciting times I had experienced in all the various places where I had served. My father said he had to work hard during the war to keep the shop going and had been told he had a heart condition and so should take things easy so he had decided to become semi-retired and try to be elected to Stranraer Town Council. That suited me. At ten o'clock father and I went down to the shop to have a look around. I saw some things that needed to be done so started to work.

This began another stage of my life. In a very short time I realised that I was not happy at home. There was little new furniture to sell; the shop was kept open by sale of second-hand goods and repairs.

I had no friends and missed the companionship and wondered if I could get back into the Air Force. Then a letter arrived asking for further details of father's condition, with the option of re-enlistment until I was due to be demobbed. I decided to return to the Air Force and try to be promoted. I was sent to North Weald near Epping, not far from London.

When I arrived at RAF North Weald in the summer of 1946 I had an interview with the Adjutant who asked me what I would like to do. He said that I could be the station signals officer or the warrant officer in charge of the barrack stores. I chose to be in charge of the barrack stores. I had to take my orders from a Squadron Leader to whom I had to report every Thursday morning. In the office I had two civilians who were retired warrant officers and one ACW2 WAAF. I had a sergeant who had ten AC2s and a Bedford lorry and was in charge of the coal for heating the station. As well as being in charge of the people issuing items from the barrack store one of my responsibilities was to ensure that a row of married quarters was cleaned up and furnished ready for occupation and for this I had a squad of twelve German POWs. Everyone worked together well and I didn't have very much trouble with anyone. I was given a bike to use which was very handy to cycle round the station. I found that

*Time for a siesta between flights.*

I was being given more and more tasks to do but to make up for this the Squadron Leader gave me another WAAF to help. It was very pleasant to be at North Weald. I liked the friendly atmosphere and the job I had to do. The Sergeants' Mess was what it should be and the meals were excellent. Although I approached the Squadron Leader to ask about promotion he said that with my qualifications as a WOP/AG I would need to retrain into another trade and accept a lower rank. This was unacceptable. Eventually the time came for me to be demobbed finally. I said goodbye to my staff who had worked with me during the last few months and to the pals I had made on the station. Then, on 30th October, 1946, aged 23, I was demobbed the second time and came away with another demob suit. Then I got onto the Paddy and returned to Stranraer with the aim of helping to build up the furniture business.

After being demobbed I returned to the furniture business and it flourished. I married and have a daughter and two fine grandsons. During my business years I was honoured by being elected President of the Glasgow and West of Scotland House Furnishers Association for three years and was on the council of the Scottish Furniture Trades Benevolent Association. I sold my two shops in Newton Stewart and retired in 1998. I am a member of Rotary, Probus and the Air Crew Association and have been an elder in our church for over 40 years. I feel that I have lived a full and enjoyable life and am still quite fit and well.

I am immensely proud that, during the war, I flew with the air force against the enemy and can be numbered with all of those who played their part in WW2. I will finish up with the well-known words from Tennyson's Ulysses.

*...you and I are old;*
*Old age hath yet his honour and his toil;*
*Death closes all: but something ere the end,*
*Some work of noble note, may yet be done,*
*Not unbecoming men that strove with gods.*

This book has been published by Stranraer and District Local History Trust which was constituted in 1998 at the instigation of the Stranraer and District Chamber of Commerce.

Previous Trust Publications:

Stranraer in World War Two
— Archie Bell.

The Loss of the Princess Victoria
— Jack Hunter.

The Cairnryan Military Railway 1941-1959
— Bill Gill.

A Peep at Stranraer's Past
— Donnie Nelson.

Royal Burgh of Stranraer - 1617-1967-2000
— John S. Boyd, Jack Hunter, Donnie Nelson, Christine L. Wilson.

Don't Plague the Ferryman
— Trevor Boult.

Portpatrick to Donaghadee
— Fraser G. MacHaffie.

The Rhins Forgotten Air Disaster
— Sandy Rankin.

Place Names in the Rhinns of Galloway and Luce Valley
— Prof. John MacQueen.

Auld Lang Syne in the Rhins of Galloway
— Prof. Charles McNeil.

The Lost Town of Innermessan
— Jack Hunter.

Every Beach a Port
— Bill McCormack.

# Trust Membership 2006

Mrs Sheelagh Afia
Mr Peter Armitage
Mrs Elaine Barton
Mr Archie Bell
Mrs Dorothy Bell
Mr Douglas Brown
Mr David B. Cairns
Mr John Cameron
Mrs Pat Cameron
Mr John Carruth
Mr Charles Collins
Mrs Harriet Collins
Mrs Marion Cunningham
Mr J. P. Davis
Mr Bill Dougan
Mr Jim Ferguson
Mr Norman Fidler
Mr C. J. Findlay
Miss Dora Gorman
Mrs Irene Grant
Mrs Gil Gray
Mr Tom Hargreaves
Mrs A. C. Harkness
Mr John Harkness
Mrs M. J. Heaney
Mr W. A. Heaney
Mr Richard Holme
Mr Peter Holmes
Mr Jack Hunter
Mr P. H. K. Lilley
Mr Robert Lindsay
Mrs Margaret MacArthur
Mrs Rosemary McCormack
Mr Colin McCubbin
Mrs Irene McKie
Mrs Nancy McLucas
Prof. John MacQueen, *Vice-Chairman*
Mrs Winifred MacQueen
Mrs Margaret Matthews
Mr Harry Monteith
Mr Alasdair Morgan
Mrs Lynn Neild
Mr Donnie Nelson MBE, *Chairman*
Mrs Mae Nelson
Mrs Helen Nish
Mr Alastair Penman
Mr John Pickin
Mr Jim Pratt
Mrs Margaret Pratt
Mr Jim Rafferty
Mrs Helen Scott
Mr Tom A. Sexton
Mr J. D. Sharp
Mr P. N. Skinner
Mrs Renee Smith
Mr Bill Stanley
Mr D. G. Start
Mrs Sheila Stevenson
Mr Tom Stevenson, *Treasurer*
Mr James Stewart
Mr Russell Walker
Mr David Williamson
Mr David Willison
Mrs Christine Wilson, *Secretary*
Mrs Elizabeth Wilson
Mr Eric Wilson
Mr William Wilson

**Stranraer & District Group for Economic Growth and Regeneration**